UNUSUAL LiFe CYCLES OF

REPTILES

by Jaclyn Jaycox

CAPSTONE PRESS
a capstone imprint

Capstone Captivate is published by Capstone Press, an imprint of Capstone.
1710 Roe Crest Drive
North Mankato, Minnesota 56003
www.capstonepub.com

Library of Congress Cataloging-in-Publication Data is available on the Library of Congress website.
ISBN: 978-1-4966-9561-1 (hardcover)
ISBN: 978-1-4966-9704-2 (paperback)
ISBN: 978-1-9771-5526-9 (eBook PDF)

Summary:
Have you ever heard of a reptile that spends most of its life in an egg? What about a reptile that has to lay its eggs on the same beach where it was hatched? Young readers will learn all about Madagascar chameleons, sea turtles, and other reptiles with unusual life cycles.

Image Credits
Shutterstock: BeautilBlossoms, 9, Catchlight Lens, 15, cems77, 19, Damsea, 27, Don Mammoser, 17, dwi putra stock, 23, Elvin A. Santana, 5, Jan Bures, 13, Jennah Vaughn, 29, Kazakova Maryia, 7, Rich Carey, cover, 25, Sean Lema, 21, Victor Suarez Naranjo, 11

Design elements: Shutterstock: emEF, Max Krasnov

Editorial Credits
Editor: Gena Chester; Designer: Bobbie Nuytten; Media Researcher: Kelly Garvin; Production Specialist: Laura Manthe

All internet sites appearing in back matter were available and accurate when this book was sent to press.

Words in **bold** are in the glossary.

Printed and Bound in China. PO4205

Table of Contents

CHAPTER 1

Reptile Life Cycle

Reptiles are some of the oldest kinds of animals on Earth. They have been around for more than 300 million years. There are more than 8,000 types of reptiles. Turtles, snakes, lizards, alligators, and crocodiles are all reptiles.

Reptiles have many things in common. They all have scales. They lay eggs. They are cold-blooded. This means if it's cold out, reptiles are cold. If it's hot outside, they are hot.

Most reptiles have the same life cycle. For example, turtles start out life as eggs. The parents leave their eggs after laying them. Turtle eggs usually hatch after a month or two. Newborn turtles are called hatchlings.

A sea turtle hatching from its egg

Hatchlings can swim and walk within the first couple hours of life. They have no parents to care for them. They have to survive on their own. The hatchlings look like miniature adults. As they grow, they go through a juvenile stage of life. They are no longer babies, but not quite adults. The adult stage is reached when the turtles are ready to **reproduce**.

This is the life cycle most reptiles go through. But there are a few reptiles that do things a bit differently. Some give birth to live babies. Others stay with their eggs to protect their young. And some live very short or very long lives.

BOYS OR GIRLS?

For many reptiles, the temperature of their eggs determines if the hatchlings will be male or female. If turtle eggs are cooler, the hatchlings will be male. If the eggs are in a warmer nest, they will be female. For crocodiles, warm and cool eggs will create females. To have males, the eggs must be at an in-between temperature.

A TURTLE'S LIFE CYCLE

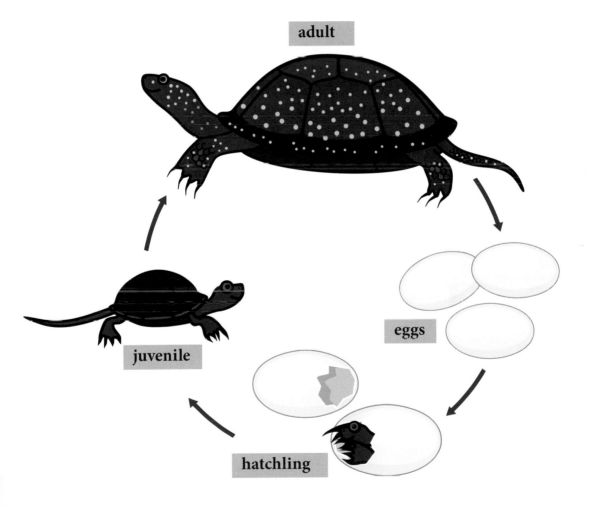

adult

eggs

hatchling

juvenile

CHAPTER 2

Unusual Life Spans

Tuataras

Tuataras are one of the most unique animals in the world. Their ancestors were part of a family of animals that lived about 200 million years ago. All other animals in this family have died out. Tuataras are the only surviving members.

Tuataras are one of the slowest growing reptiles. They aren't able to reproduce until they are between 10 and 20 years old. Females lay eggs every two to five years. They lay eggs in **burrows**. Then the females leave. The burrows are covered to protect the eggs from **predators**. The eggs are on their own.

A tuatara

Tuatara eggs take up to 15 months to hatch. This is one of the longest **incubation periods** of any reptile. When they finally hatch, the hatchlings start searching for food and digging small burrows for shelter. Young tuataras are active during the day to avoid the adults. Adult tuataras hunt for food at night. They eat mainly bugs, such as beetles, worms, and spiders. But they will also eat young tuataras.

Young tuataras grow until they are about 35 years old. They live an average of 60 years in the wild. Some have lived more than 100 years.

Fact!

Tuataras have a third eye. Scientists aren't sure what it is used for. Some believe the extra eye might help tuataras tell the time of day and season.

A tuatara in its burrow

Madagascar Chameleons

Chameleons from Madagascar spend most of their lives in eggs. They have a faster growth rate and shorter life span than any other four-legged animal. Females lay their eggs at the end of the wet season in January and February. They cover them with sand. Then they and all other adult chameleons die. The eggs wait out the dry season and hatch about eight months later during the wet season.

The young chameleons spend all of their time eating spiders and other insects. They grow very quickly. Females turn bright colors to attract males. After two months of life, they are ready to **mate**. The females lay their eggs to repeat the life cycle. In all, they live four to five months.

A Madagascar chameleon

CHAPTER 3

Protective Parents

Crocodiles

Crocodiles are found in **tropical** areas in Australia, Africa, Asia, and the U.S. They live near lakes and rivers. After mating, a female makes a nest. Some types of crocodiles dig holes in the sand. Others build nests out of leaves and sticks. The female lays between 30 and 60 eggs. Then she covers them to keep the eggs warm.

Crocodile eggs and young crocodiles have a number of predators. Instead of leaving the eggs, the female guards the nest. The male protects the female and nest. When the eggs start to hatch, the babies chirp. Their mother digs them out. She carries them in her mouth to the water. The mother protects her young for weeks or sometimes months to keep them safe. Crocodiles can live up to 75 years.

A female crocodile taking her hatchling to the water

Komodo Dragons

Komodo dragons live in tropical areas. These places have a dry season and a wet season. Mating happens toward the end of the dry season.

A female digs a hole in the ground for a nest. She lays about 30 eggs and covers them with dirt and leaves. She then guards the nest from predators such as wild dogs and other Komodo dragons. The female spends almost all of her time there. After a few months, the female leaves. From then on, the eggs will be on their own.

Fact!

Komodo dragons are the largest lizards in the world. The biggest one recorded was 10.3 feet (3.1 meters) long and weighed 366 pounds (166 kilograms)!

A Komodo dragon leaving its nest

When Komodo dragons hatch, they dig their way to the surface. They run to trees and climb up for safety. Adult Komodo dragons may try to eat them! Hatchlings can be green, yellow, brown, or gray. Their coloring helps them blend in with the trees. Young dragons live in trees until they are big enough to defend themselves against predators.

Komodo dragons live alone in the wild. A female doesn't always find a male to mate. She can still lay eggs without mating. This ensures Komodo dragons are able to repeat their life cycle. There are very few animals that have this ability. In fact, only 0.1 percent of **vertebrates** can do this.

A Komodo dragon hatchling in a tree, safe from predators

CHAPTER 4

Girls Only

Whiptail Lizards

Like Komodo dragons, some kinds of whiptail lizards can reproduce without mating. Unlike Komodo dragons, it doesn't happen because males can't be found. It happens because there are no males! Some kinds of whiptail lizards have entire populations that are only females.

These female whiptail lizards are able to make copies of themselves. This is called **cloning**. The hatchlings are exactly like their mothers. About a year or two after hatching, these whiptail lizards are ready to lay cloned eggs of their own.

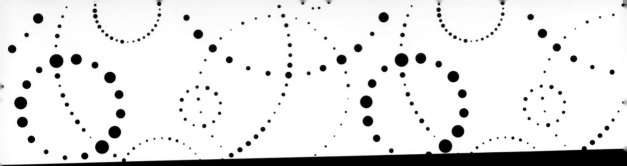

A whiptail lizard in New Mexico

CHAPTER 5

Strange Births

Blue-Tongued Skinks

The blue-tongued skink is a type of lizard. It has shiny scales and a bright blue tongue. It usually lives alone, only coming together to mate. Unlike other reptiles, the blue-tongued skink doesn't lay eggs. The female carries the eggs inside her for about three months. The eggs hatch while still inside her. Then she gives birth to up to 20 live babies.

The hatchlings are on their own after birth. They spend their days looking for food. They hide under leaves at night for shelter. When predators come near, they stick out their bright blue tongues. Bright colors usually mean an animal is poisonous. These lizards are not, but their tongues trick predators long enough for them to escape. Blue-tongued skinks become adults after about three years. They can live at least 20 years.

SOLOMON ISLANDS SKINKS

Solomon Islands skinks also give birth to live young. But they reproduce very slowly. They usually have only one baby at a time. It develops for six to eight months before being born. The baby is huge! It can be almost half the size of its mother.

A blue-tongued skink shows its tongue to scare off a predator.

CHAPTER 6

From Land to Water

Banded Sea Kraits

Banded sea kraits are a type of sea snake. Most sea snakes live their whole lives in the water. But banded sea kraits spend nearly half of their time on land. They hunt for eels in the ocean. Even though the eels are much larger than the sea kraits, they swallow the eels whole. Eating such a big meal makes it hard for the sea kraits to swim. They must come to land to **digest** their food. It can take several weeks.

Banded sea kraits are built for life on land and underwater. They have large scales on their bellies. The scales help them move more easily on land and climb trees for shelter. Most other sea snakes cannot move at all on land. Banded sea kraits are also able to stay underwater for up to 30 minutes without taking a breath. Their noses and mouths seal shut when they are in the water.

A banded sea krait

Banded sea kraits also come to land to mate. Females lay their eggs in the sand or in the cracks of rocks. The placement keeps the eggs hidden from predators. Some types of sea kraits can lay up to 20 eggs at once. The eggs hatch after at least four months. The young sea kraits find their way to the water.

Banded sea kraits reach adulthood at about 18 months. When they are ready to reproduce, they often return to the same beach where they were born. Some travel long distances to get back there.

A banded sea krait on land

Sea Turtles

Sea turtles spend most of their lives in the ocean. But they come to shore to lay their eggs. Females dig holes in the sand. They lay their eggs and cover them. This protects them from predators such as raccoons, foxes, snakes, and lizards. Then the females head back into the water.

A few weeks later, the eggs hatch. The hatchlings dig their way out of the sand and make their way to the ocean. The ocean **currents** can carry the babies thousands of miles away. They spend between 10 and 50 years at sea before they are able to mate. Adult sea turtles travel back to the nesting area where they were born to lay their eggs. No other reptile travels such distances to lay eggs. Sea turtles can live up to 100 years.

Fact!

Sea turtles can travel long distances. Scientists tracked one turtle that traveled from California to Japan. It swam more than 9,000 miles (14,500 kilometers)!

Newly hatched sea turtles making their way to the ocean

Glossary

burrow (BUHR-oh)—a hole in the ground made or used by an animal; also, to dig

clone (KLOHN)—to use an animal's cells to grow another identical animal

current (KUHR-unt)—the movement of water in a river or an ocean

digest (dy-GEST)—to break down food so it can be used by the body

incubation period (in-cyoo-BAY-shuhn PEER-ee-id)—the time it takes for eggs to hatch

mate (MATE)—to join with another to produce young

predator (PRED-uh-tur)—an animal that hunts other animals for food

reproduce (ree-pruh-DOOSE)—to make offspring

reptile (REP-tile)—a cold-blooded animal that breathes air and has a backbone; most reptiles have scales

tropical (TRAH-pi-kuhl)—hot and wet; places near the equator are tropical

vertebrate (VUR-tuh-brayt)—an animal with a backbone

Read More

Jacobson, Bray. *Reptile Life Cycles*. New York: Gareth Stevens Publishing, 2018.

Owings, Lisa. *From Egg to Sea Turtle*. Minneapolis: Lerner Publishing, 2017.

Ringstad, Arnold. *Totally Amazing Facts About Reptiles*. North Mankato, MN: Capstone Press, 2018.

Internet Sites

Britannica Kids: Reptiles
kids.britannica.com/students/article/reptiles/276696

Cool Kid Facts: Crocodiles
coolkidfacts.com/crocodile-facts/

National Geographic Kids: Green Sea Turtles
kids.nationalgcographic.com/animals/reptiles/green-sea-turtle/

Index